Test # 0.668

R.L.   5.9

Pts.   0.5

A History of
Sailing Ships

MOVING PEOPLE, THINGS, AND IDEAS

Other Books in the Series

MOVING PEOPLE, THINGS, AND IDEAS

A HISTORY OF SAILING SHIPS

Text by Renzo Rossi

BLACKBIRCH PRESS

An imprint of Thomson Gale, a part of The Thomson Corporation

THOMSON

GALE

Detroit • New York • San Francisco • San Diego • New Haven, Conn. • Waterville, Maine • London • Munich

Copyright © 2004 by Andrea Dué s.r.l., Florence, Italy

Published in 2006 in North America by Thomson Gale

All rights reserved

Conception and production: Andrea Dué s.r.l.
Text: Renzo Rossi
Translation: Erika Pauli
Illustrations: Alessandro Baldanzi, Alessandro Bartolozzi, Leonello Calvetti, Lorenzo Cecchi, Sauro
Giampaia, Luigi Ieracitano, Roberto Simoni, Studio Stalio (Alessandro Cantucci)
Research, documentation, and layout: Luigi Ieracitano
Cutouts: Uliana Derniatina

Thomson and Star Logo are trademarks and Gale and Blackbirch Press are registered trademarks used herein under license.

For more information, contact
Blackbirch Press
27500 Drake Rd.
Farmington Hills, MI 48331-3535
Or you can visit our Internet site at http://www.gale.com

LIBRARY OF CONGRESS CATALOGING-IN-PUBLICATION DATA

Rossi, Renzo, 1940–
  A history of sailing ships / by Renzo Rossi.
     p. cm. — (Moving people, things, and ideas)
  Includes bibliographical references and index.
  ISBN 1-4103-0661-5 (hardcover : alk. paper) 1. Sailing ships—History—Juvenile
literature. I. Title. II. Series.
  VM150.R6279 2005
  623.82'03—dc22
                                                                    2005007157

Printed in the United States
10 9 8 7 6 5 4 3 2 1

Contents

Early Sailing Ships

The oldest drawings of boats come from Mesopotamia and Egypt. They date between 4000 and 3000 B.C. But scientists believe that some people were making long voyages much earlier. Those who wanted to use boats to trade goods with others had to learn many skills. For one, they needed to learn how to make boats that were sturdy enough for long journeys in rough seas. They had to find or buy the materials needed to build these ships. Then they had to decide what goods to send and where to send them. Once it was decided who would buy the goods, they needed to learn to trade or sell their own goods and buy others. They also had to make sure they had safe places to moor, or secure, their boats. They did this by improving natural coves or building ports.

Early civilizations that developed sailing ships include the Egyptians, the Minoans, the Phoenicians, and the Greeks. The Egyptians, for example, sailed up and down the Nile River, and in time they went as far as the Red Sea.

Above: A drawing shows an ancient Egyptian ship used for transportation on the Nile River. It had a large, long-handled steering oar at the stern, or back of the ship.

Below: Carvings from the 8th century B.C. show Phoenician ships towing tree trunks. The prow (front part of the ship) is carved with a horse's head. The Greeks called this kind of boat a "hippo." _Hippo_ was the ancient Greek word for "horse."

Below: A drawing shows Minoan ships on a beach.

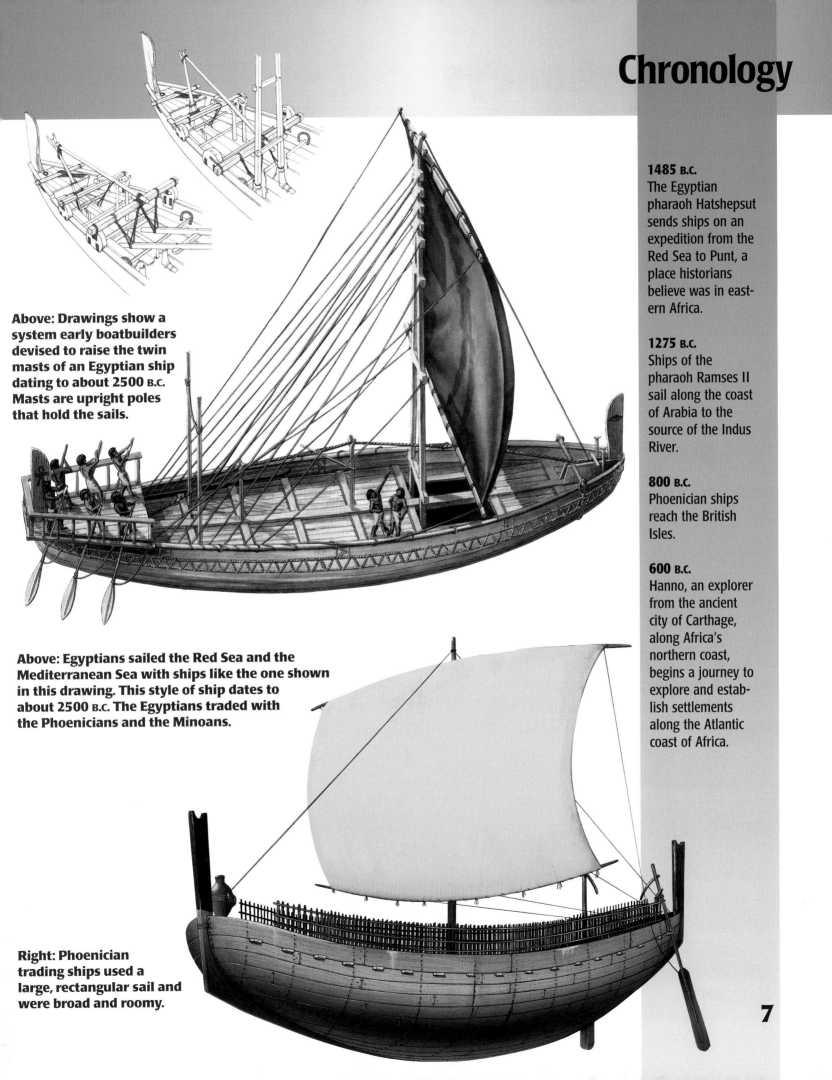

Chronology

Above: Drawings show a system early boatbuilders devised to raise the twin masts of an Egyptian ship dating to about 2500 B.C. Masts are upright poles that hold the sails.

Above: Egyptians sailed the Red Sea and the Mediterranean Sea with ships like the one shown in this drawing. This style of ship dates to about 2500 B.C. The Egyptians traded with the Phoenicians and the Minoans.

Right: Phoenician trading ships used a large, rectangular sail and were broad and roomy.

1485 B.C.
The Egyptian pharaoh Hatshepsut sends ships on an expedition from the Red Sea to Punt, a place historians believe was in eastern Africa.

1275 B.C.
Ships of the pharaoh Ramses II sail along the coast of Arabia to the source of the Indus River.

800 B.C.
Phoenician ships reach the British Isles.

600 B.C.
Hanno, an explorer from the ancient city of Carthage, along Africa's northern coast, begins a journey to explore and establish settlements along the Atlantic coast of Africa.

Ancient Galleys

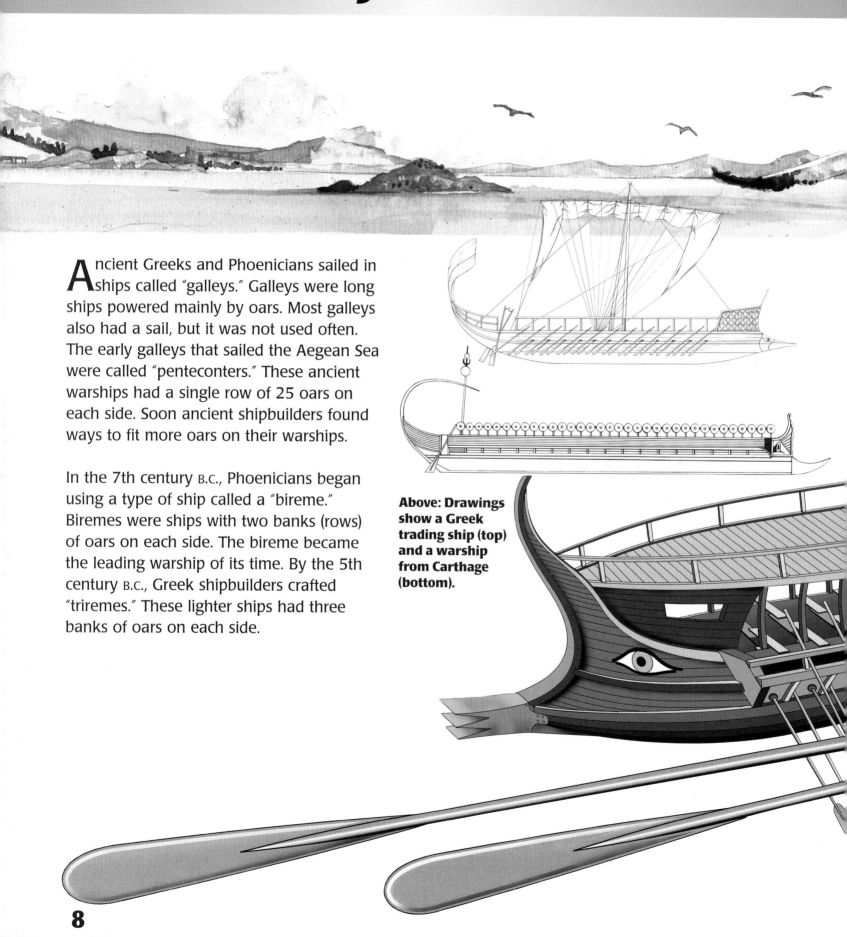

Ancient Greeks and Phoenicians sailed in ships called "galleys." Galleys were long ships powered mainly by oars. Most galleys also had a sail, but it was not used often. The early galleys that sailed the Aegean Sea were called "penteconters." These ancient warships had a single row of 25 oars on each side. Soon ancient shipbuilders found ways to fit more oars on their warships.

In the 7th century B.C., Phoenicians began using a type of ship called a "bireme." Biremes were ships with two banks (rows) of oars on each side. The bireme became the leading warship of its time. By the 5th century B.C., Greek shipbuilders crafted "triremes." These lighter ships had three banks of oars on each side.

Above: Drawings show a Greek trading ship (top) and a warship from Carthage (bottom).

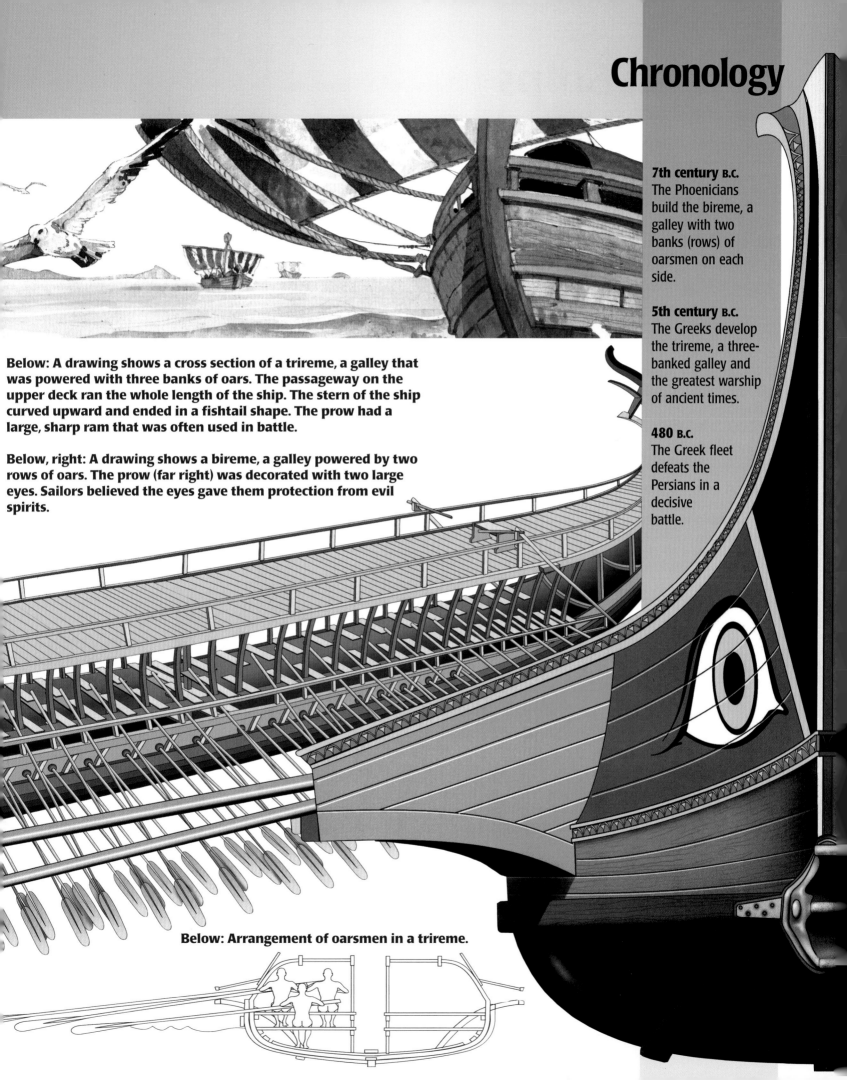

Chronology

Below: A drawing shows a cross section of a trireme, a galley that was powered with three banks of oars. The passageway on the upper deck ran the whole length of the ship. The stern of the ship curved upward and ended in a fishtail shape. The prow had a large, sharp ram that was often used in battle.

Below, right: A drawing shows a bireme, a galley powered by two rows of oars. The prow (far right) was decorated with two large eyes. Sailors believed the eyes gave them protection from evil spirits.

Below: Arrangement of oarsmen in a trireme.

Roman Ships

In war, ancient Romans relied far more on their army than on their navy. But during the First Punic War with Carthage, which began in 264 B.C., the Romans needed to put together a fleet of ships quickly. The ships they built were modeled on those the Greeks had used in earlier times. But the Roman ships had a new invention called a "grappling spike." This device allowed them to attach a gangplank from their ship to an enemy's ship. The Romans defeated Carthage in 241 B.C.

Opposite, above: A drawing shows a Roman warship with a hinged gangplank. When the gangplank was let down, a grappling spike, called a "corvus," fastened onto the deck of the enemy's ship. This let soldiers board an enemy ship.

Opposite, center: A drawing shows the large, hexagon-shaped basin the Roman emperor Trajan ordered excavated to improve the harbor of Ostia, near Rome. The sides were lined with warehouses for wheat that was shipped from Africa on cargo vessels.

Opposite, below: A drawing shows a Byzantine war dromon from the late 12th century. The dromon was a fast ship because of its many oars; its full, triangular sail; and its slender hull (the frame or body of the ship).

Below: A drawing shows a Roman merchantman, as this type of ship was called. It had a high cabin on its deck and a square sail on a single mast.

Left: A drawing of an anchor used by Roman ships. The anchors were made of iron and then covered in wood. The points of the anchor were made of lead.

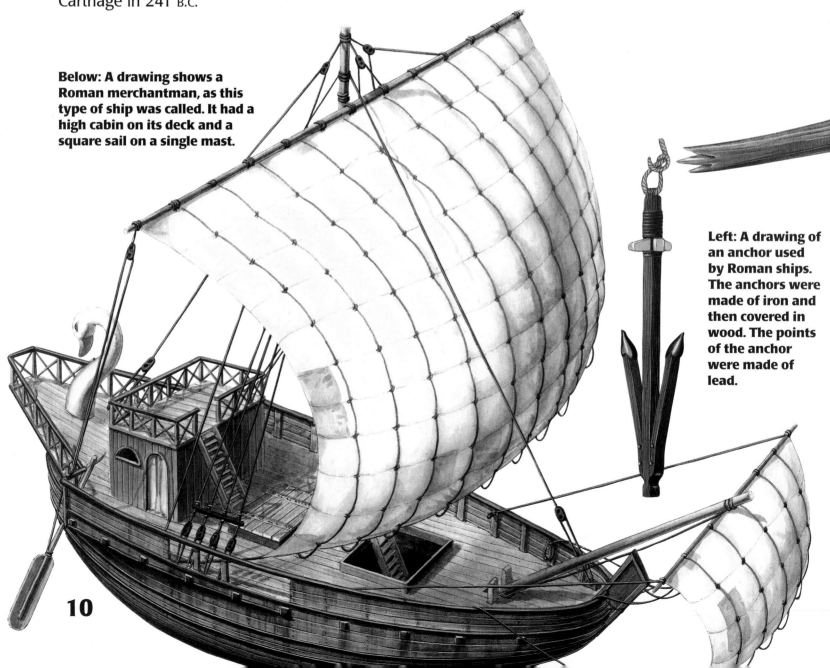

260 B.C.
Rome wins its first great naval victory against Carthage.

67 B.C.
Gnaeus Pompeius Magnus, the Roman military leader known as Pompey the Great, defeats the pirates who controlled the Mediterranean Sea.

31 B.C.
The Roman emperor Caesar Augustus creates a permanent military fleet based at Miseno, near Naples, Italy, and at Ravenna, in Italy, on the Adriatic Sea.

A.D. 41–54
Under the Roman emperor Claudius, Ostia becomes an international port.

A.D. 112
The Roman emperor Trajan enlarges the port of Ostia.

Viking Ships

The Viking Age refers to the time from about A.D. 790 to about A.D. 1050. Vikings were explorers who came from what is now Scandinavia. They explored and raided parts of Europe, the Middle East, northern Africa, and even North America.

The Vikings used shipbuilding techniques that were the most advanced of their time. Their ships were fast and sleek. Because they were long, they were called "long ships." The long ships could travel in rough ocean waters, in shallow coastal areas, and along rivers. The ships were pointed at both ends so that they could go forward or backward without turning around.

The Vikings improved their sailing ships by adding a keel, a long, narrow piece of wood that formed the backbone of the ship. This added feature reduced the ship's rolling motion and allowed it to go faster.

The drakkar, or the dragon ship, was one of the best-known types of Viking ship. These ships had tall, curved prows carved with dragon heads and were powered by 120 oarsmen, 60 on each side.

Right: The Oseberg ship is an example of a karv, a type of Viking ship. The karv was built of oak. It had a large sail and fifteen pairs of oars. In 1904 the Oseberg ship was excavated from a Norwegian fjord, an inlet of water. The ship had been used as a burial chamber for a woman believed to be a princess or other member of royalty during Viking times. The Oseberg ship is one of three ships on display at the Viking Ship Museum near Oslo, Norway.

Above and left:
Drawings show a
typical Viking
trading ship, called
a "knorr." Freight was
stowed on the deck
and in the deep hull.

820
Vikings land in
Ireland.

859
A Viking expedition
passes through the
Strait of Gibraltar
and enters the
Mediterranean Sea.

860
Vikings colonize
Iceland.

992
Vikings sail the
Seine River and
attack Paris.

982
Erik the Red, a
Norwegian living in
Iceland, reaches
Greenland. Over
time he convinces
several hundred
Icelanders to settle
there.

1000
Vikings land on the
North American
coastal areas of
Labrador and
Newfoundland.

In the Mediterranean and Baltic Seas

As early as the 11th century, people living in the western Mediterranean Sea region used galleys. The streamlined galleys had oars and lateen, or triangular, sails. They were the ships favored by sailing centers including Venice, Genoa, Marseilles, and Barcelona. Some galleys were also used as warships.

In the 13th century, a group of trading cities in northern Europe formed the Hanseatic League. At its peak, the league consisted of merchants from more than 160 cities and towns who banded together to dominate trade in the Baltic Sea. The ship commonly used in the region at the time was called a "cog." Cogs were large merchant ships that were most likely designed in Germany. Cogs had high sides, a flat bottom, and one square sail.

Top: A drawing of an Arab ship dates from a 13th-century manuscript.

Center: Art from 12th-century Venice shows sailors transporting religious items on a ship with three masts and two rudders.

Right: This drawing of a 13th-century merchant ship from Pisa shows raised areas called "castles" on the prow and stern above the deck.

In the background: A drawing shows a 13th-century ship with a castle placed high above the hull.

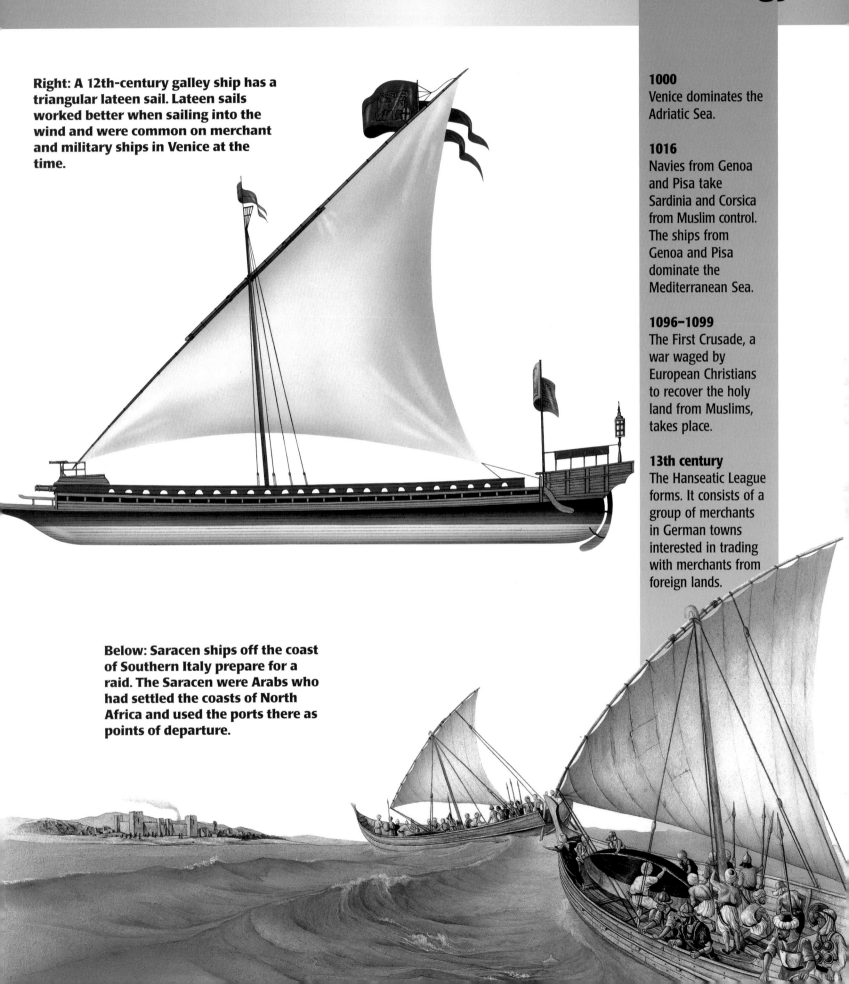

Right: A 12th-century galley ship has a triangular lateen sail. Lateen sails worked better when sailing into the wind and were common on merchant and military ships in Venice at the time.

Below: Saracen ships off the coast of Southern Italy prepare for a raid. The Saracen were Arabs who had settled the coasts of North Africa and used the ports there as points of departure.

1000
Venice dominates the Adriatic Sea.

1016
Navies from Genoa and Pisa take Sardinia and Corsica from Muslim control. The ships from Genoa and Pisa dominate the Mediterranean Sea.

1096–1099
The First Crusade, a war waged by European Christians to recover the holy land from Muslims, takes place.

13th century
The Hanseatic League forms. It consists of a group of merchants in German towns interested in trading with merchants from foreign lands.

The Cog

The cog gradually replaced the Viking long ships as the dominant type of ship on the seas of northern Europe through the early 1400s. It was wide and spacious, and early versions had open hulls. Cogs built later were larger. They had decks and used a rudder to steer instead of oars. They also had raised platforms at the prow and stern called "castles." One castle was used for warfare and the other to shelter important guests. Scientists learned much of what they know about cogs after the wrecked hull of a cog built in 1380 was found when workers were dredging the Weser River near Bremen, Germany. It took seven years to restore the ship.

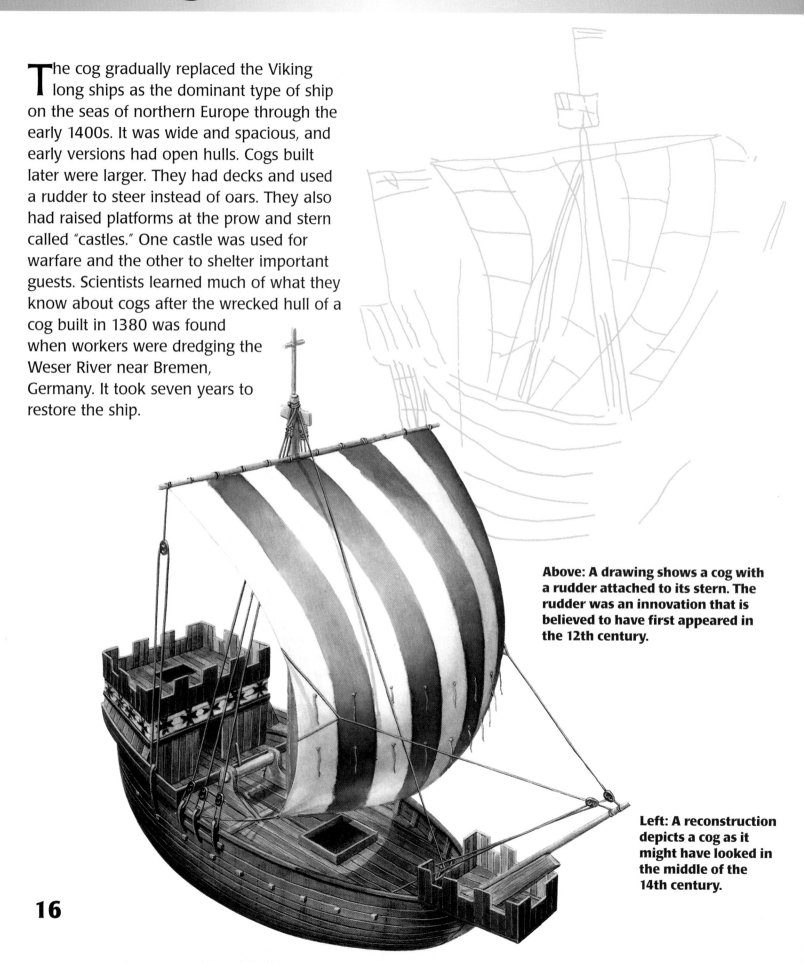

Above: A drawing shows a cog with a rudder attached to its stern. The rudder was an innovation that is believed to have first appeared in the 12th century.

Left: A reconstruction depicts a cog as it might have looked in the middle of the 14th century.

1304
Leding, a Danish naval organization, adopts the cog as its preferred ship design.

1310
Shipbuilders in Venice and Genoa copy the Nordic cog design.

1336
Written materials first mention the use of artillery onboard a ship.

Above: A 14th-century drawing shows cogs sailing on the sea.

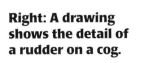

Right: A drawing shows the detail of a rudder on a cog.

The Carrack

At the beginning of the 15th century, another type of merchant ship, called a "carrack," began to sail on the Mediterranean Sea. Carracks were similar to cogs, but they were larger. They also had more masts and added a triangular sail. Carracks carried a large crew, provisions, and cargo. They also had huge castles with many decks and carried weapons. This made carracks useful as warships.

Right: A drawing shows a reconstruction of a carrack in a style that was common in the middle of the 15th century. The model is based on a carrack that was recovered.

1367
A carrack is depicted on a map for the first time.

1400
The carrack begins replacing the cog as the most common type of ship on the seas.

1492
The *Santa Maria*, a carrack, is one of three ships that sailed to the New World with Christopher Columbus.

1519
Portuguese explorer Ferdinand Magellan begins his journey around the world with five carracks.

Above: A reconstruction shows how a carrack of the late 15th century might have looked. The combination of a large square sail and a smaller triangular sail helped the ship sail the Atlantic Ocean.

Left: A late 18th-century drawing shows a ship with two sails that was used in the Mediterranean Sea.

Maps and Navigation Instruments

Sailing in ancient times was difficult, and sometimes frightening, because it was very hard for sailors to know where they were. For a long time, sailors sailed only where they could stay in sight of land. Over time, people began to invent tools that helped them find their way at sea.

One of the tools they devised was a nautical chart called a "portolano." The name *portolano* is Italian and refers to written sailing directions. The portolano became an important guide between the 14th and early 17th centuries. The portolano was a harbor-finding manual for the Middle Ages. Sailors using it could learn about the features of coasts, ports, and landings. It also helped sailors locate possible obstacles and find rivers and springs where they could get freshwater.

People also invented instruments that used the stars or the sun to help them find their location at sea, or navigate. One of the most important navigation instruments was the compass, which helped sailors identify directions. The magnetic needle on a compass always points north because of the magnetic pull from Earth's North Pole. The compass was first used in ancient China. Most sailors used it in the 11th and 12th centuries. It made sea travel safer and easier.

Below: A nautical map (portolano) of the Mediterranean.

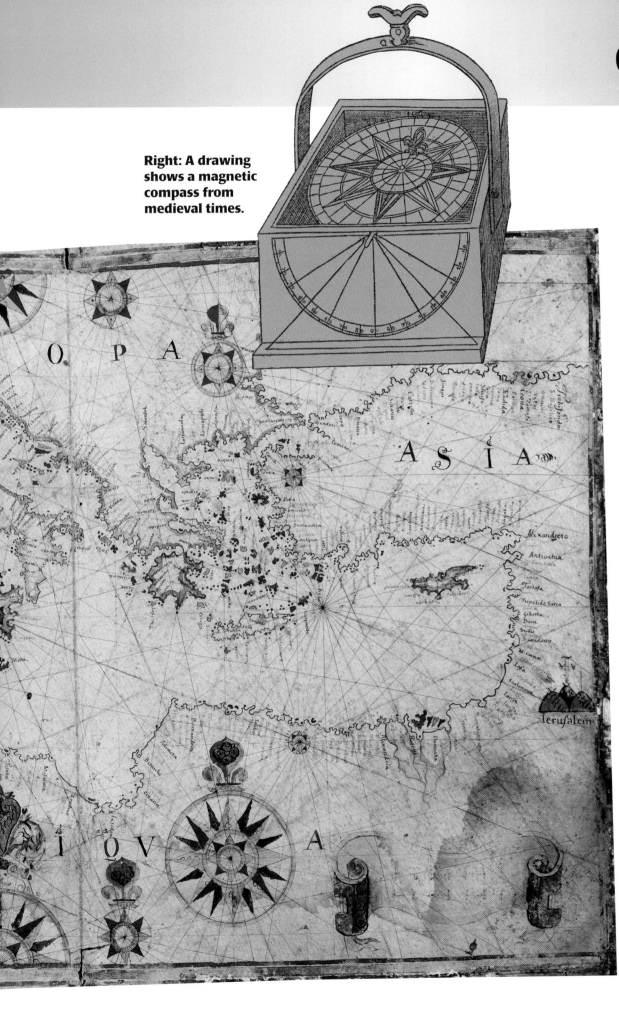

Right: A drawing shows a magnetic compass from medieval times.

Another important instrument for sailors long ago was the astrolabe. The astrolabe was a device that allowed people to use the location of a star, a planet, or the sun above the horizon to help them determine their location. Though no one knows who invented the astrolabe, ancient Greeks and Romans used it in the 1st century A.D. The astrolabe used a circular disk with a pointer attached at its center. The pointer was used to measure the angle of a star, a planet, or the sun along the horizon. By using the astrolabe, sailors could find their latitude. Latitude measures distance north or south of the equator. The astrolabe had other uses too. It could also be used to calculate time.

The quadrant was yet another instrument used for navigation. A quadrant was shaped like a quarter of a circle, so it looked like a very large slice of pizza. A weight on a string attached to the corner of the quadrant. Sailors used the quadrant by moving the weighted string in a way that allowed them to measure the height of a certain star above the horizon. By measuring this angle at regular intervals, sailors could find their ship's latitude.

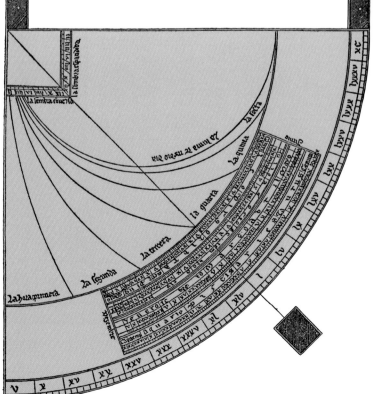

Right: A drawing shows a 15th-century quadrant.

Many details can be seen in this view of the front of an astrolabe (left) and the back (below).

1730
Englishman John Hadley invents the sextant, a device that makes use of two mirrors to measure the angle between two objects, such as a star, a planet, or the Sun and the horizon, with great accuracy. Because the sextant was more accurate for determining latitude, it replaced the astrolabe as the main instrument for navigation.

The Caravel

The carrack could carry large quantities of goods, but it was not the best choice for exploration. The caravel was the type of ship that made it possible for people to travel farther and explore the world.

No one knows just where the caravel was designed or when it was introduced. The first mention of it that historians have found dates to 1225. The caravel was a small, three-masted ship. It had a round hull and square stern. The hulls were built in a special way, with the panel of the planks on the hull touching each other but not overlapping. This style of planking was called "caravel built." The caravel design was an improvement over ships of that time. Caravels could sail very fast, and they could sail very well into the wind. They were easy to steer. Caravels also had a shallower draft that allowed them to scout a coast more easily than the carrack. A draft is the depth of a vessel's keel below the waterline.

The most famous caravels are the *Niña* and the *Pinta*, two of the three ships that Christopher Columbus took on the famous voyage from Europe to the New World in 1492.

Above: A drawing shows part of a type of map called a "planisphere." It is one of the oldest surviving maps from Europe. Martin Behaim, a geographer who worked in Portugal at the time of Columbus's 1492 expedition, created the map.

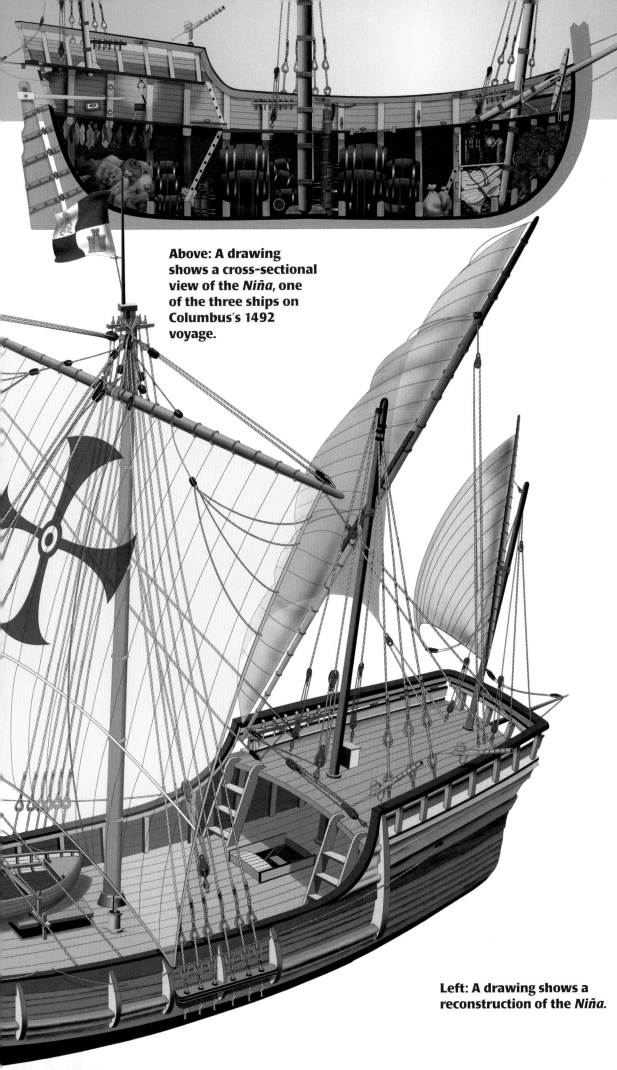

Above: A drawing shows a cross-sectional view of the *Niña*, one of the three ships on Columbus's 1492 voyage.

Early 15th century
Portuguese prince Henry the Navigator founds the world's first naval school.

1431
Portuguese explorers reach the Azores islands.

1487
Portuguese explorer Bartolomeu Dias rounds the southern coast of Africa and names it the Cape of Good Hope.

Aug. 2, 1492
Christopher Columbus sets sail from Palos, Spain.

Oct. 12, 1492
Columbus reaches the New World. Historians believe he landed in the Bahamas.

Left: A drawing shows a reconstruction of the *Niña*.

The Galleon

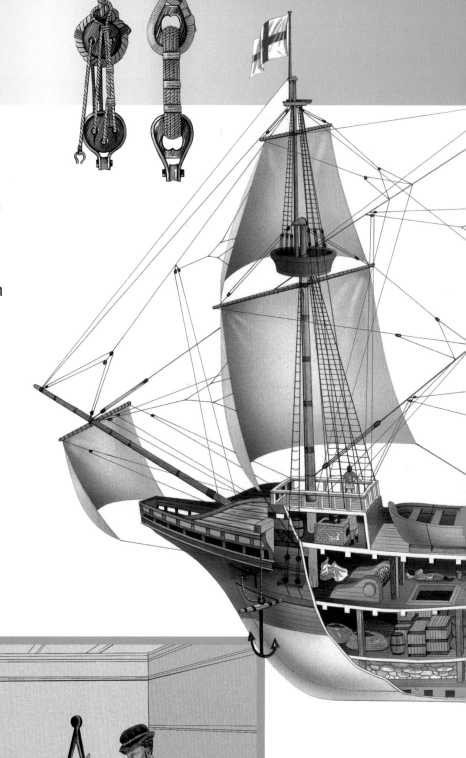

In the middle of the 16th century, a new ship called the "galleon" replaced the carracks and caravels. The galleon was used in many important battles because it was fast and powerful. Galleons were large wooden ships with slender, beaklike prows. Their sides sloped inward. This design made them more stable than earlier ship designs and allowed these warships to carry more and heavier guns. It also made it harder for an enemy to board the ship.

Galleons had three or four masts. The main deck ran the length of the hull. The crew and the ship's eating area (the galley) were in the prow. The captain's large cabin was in the back part of the ship.

Above: A drawing shows a cross section of the *Mayflower*. This galleon carried the Pilgrims to North America in 1620.

Left: A 17th-century print shows a master shipwright, as ship designers were called, working on the plans to build a galleon.

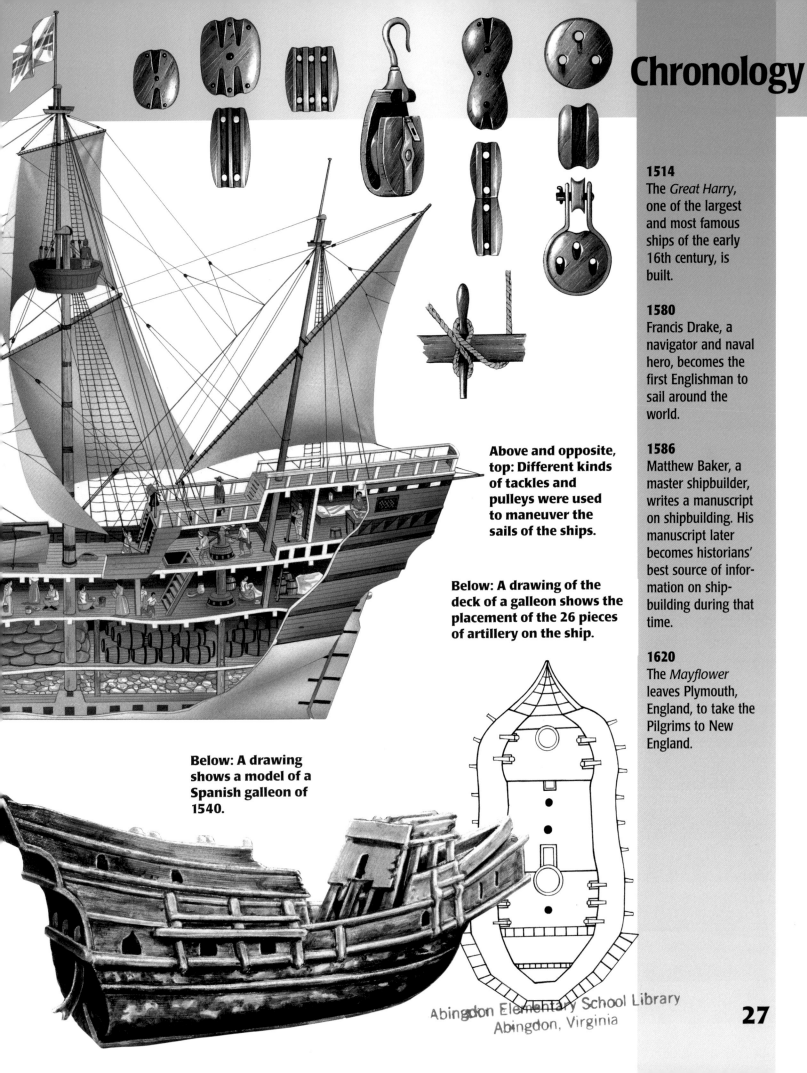

Chronology

1514
The *Great Harry*, one of the largest and most famous ships of the early 16th century, is built.

1580
Francis Drake, a navigator and naval hero, becomes the first Englishman to sail around the world.

1586
Matthew Baker, a master shipbuilder, writes a manuscript on shipbuilding. His manuscript later becomes historians' best source of information on shipbuilding during that time.

1620
The *Mayflower* leaves Plymouth, England, to take the Pilgrims to New England.

Above and opposite, top: Different kinds of tackles and pulleys were used to maneuver the sails of the ships.

Below: A drawing of the deck of a galleon shows the placement of the 26 pieces of artillery on the ship.

Below: A drawing shows a model of a Spanish galleon of 1540.

27

Battles on the Seas

In the 16th century, Spain was a world power. Its navy was called the "Invincible Armada." By that, people meant that the Spanish navy could not be defeated. In 1588 King Philip II of Spain sent the Armada out with 130 ships and 30,000 men to invade England. But the invincible fleet was destroyed by a combination of forces, including bad weather. Several thousand Spanish sailors were killed and about half of the ships in the Armada were lost. This defeat changed the way people looked at Spain and helped England rise to power.

The naval battles that led to the losses of the Spanish Armada are considered some of the first modern naval battles. Because the galleons were armed with cannons, naval captains had to change the way they waged war. Before, the only way to over-take an enemy ship had been to board it. But with cannons located along the sides of ships, fleets arranged themselves in a single line to fire at enemy ships.

main topgallant sail
topgallant mast
fore topgallant mast
fore topgallant sail
topmast
fore topmast
fore topsail
main topsail
fore spritsail
mizzen-sail
mizzen-mast
foremast
mainmast
foresail
mainsail
bowsprit
spritsail

Left: The masts and many sails of the galleon are identified in this diagram.

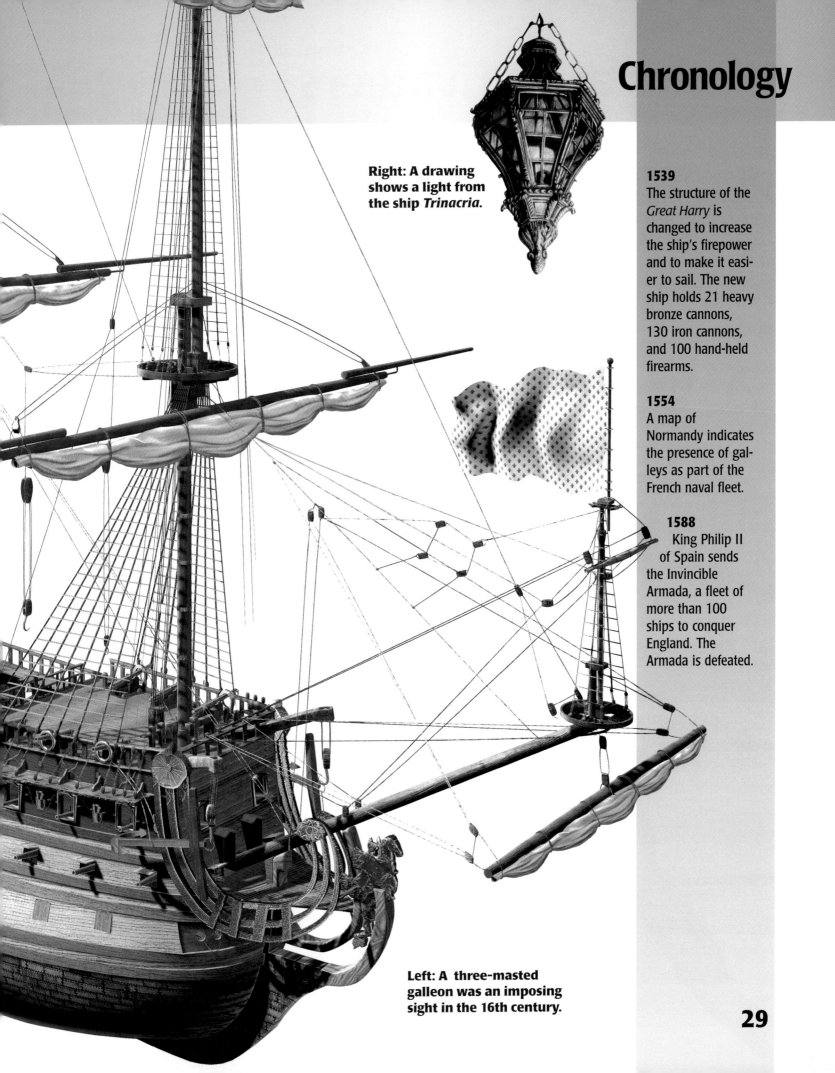

Right: A drawing shows a light from the ship _Trinacria_.

1539
The structure of the _Great Harry_ is changed to increase the ship's firepower and to make it easier to sail. The new ship holds 21 heavy bronze cannons, 130 iron cannons, and 100 hand-held firearms.

1554
A map of Normandy indicates the presence of galleys as part of the French naval fleet.

1588
King Philip II of Spain sends the Invincible Armada, a fleet of more than 100 ships to conquer England. The Armada is defeated.

Left: A three-masted galleon was an imposing sight in the 16th century.

Pirates and Privateers

Pirates were the outlaws of the sea. Pirates robbed ships at sea, or they attacked targets on shore. In the 17th century, most pirates were in the Gulf of Mexico and in the Caribbean Sea, where galleons filled with treasure sailed.

The privateer was another kind of pirate on the seas. But privateers were not outlaws. They had special licenses from governments that gave them permission to attack ships that were from enemy countries and steal their cargo. The privateers gave this cargo to their government. As payment for their services, privateers received a share of the cargo. One of the most famous privateers was Sir Francis Drake, the captain who led the British to victory over the Spanish Armada, and the first Englishman to sail around the globe.

Right: A drawing shows a device from the 18th century called a "reserve fuse." Once lit, the long fuse (wick) in the barrel continued to burn slowly in the plate below. That way it was always ready when sailors needed it.

Above right: The pirate Calico Jack used a skull over two crossed cutlasses for his ship's flag.

Far left: A drawing shows six decks toward the stern of the *Great Harry*, the best-known ship of King Henry VIII of England.

Opposite, center: Diagrams show the *Golden Hind*, Sir Francis Drake's galleon. Drake sailed around the globe in the *Golden Hind*.

Right: Pirates launched brutal attacks on ships at sea.

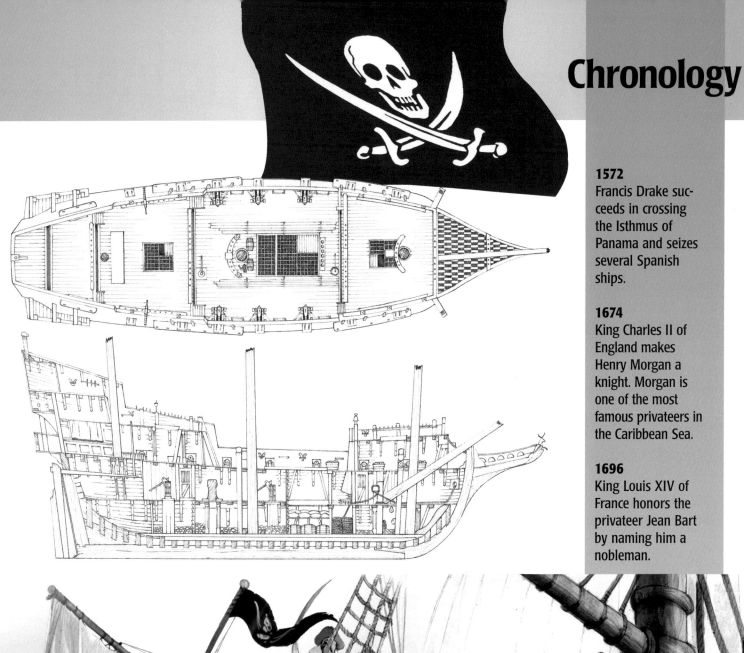

Chronology

1572
Francis Drake succeeds in crossing the Isthmus of Panama and seizes several Spanish ships.

1674
King Charles II of England makes Henry Morgan a knight. Morgan is one of the most famous privateers in the Caribbean Sea.

1696
King Louis XIV of France honors the privateer Jean Bart by naming him a nobleman.

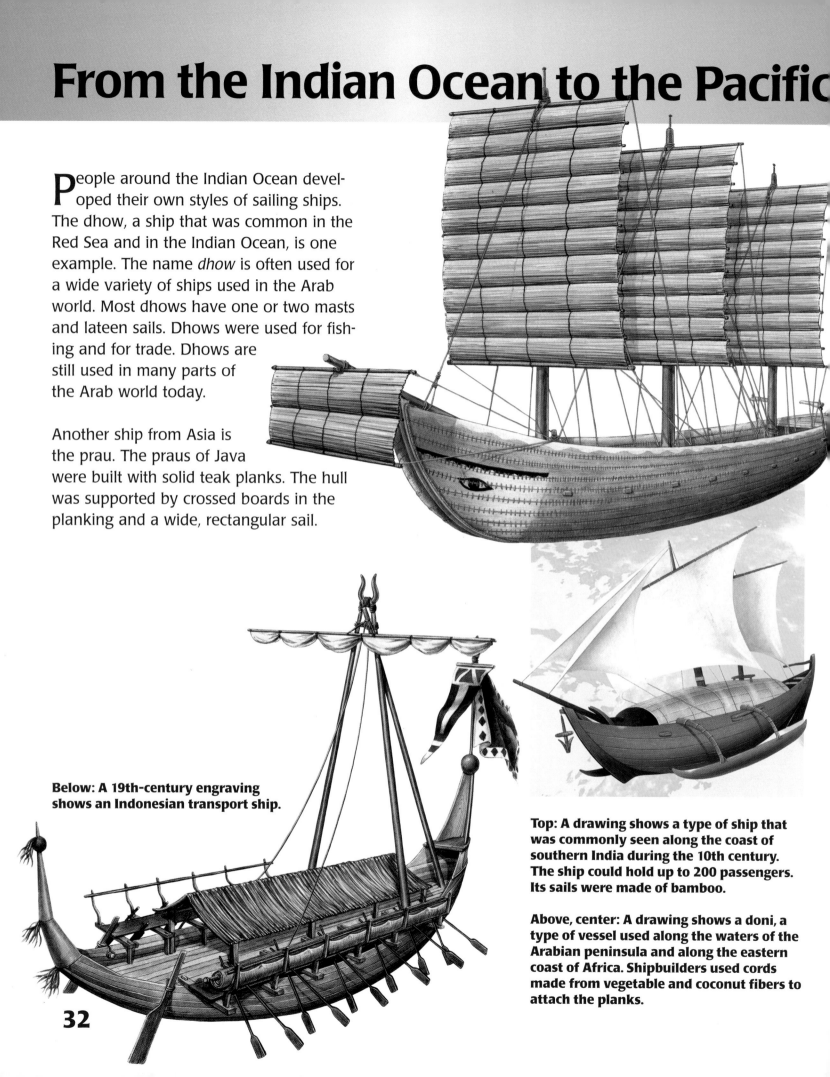

From the Indian Ocean to the Pacific

People around the Indian Ocean developed their own styles of sailing ships. The dhow, a ship that was common in the Red Sea and in the Indian Ocean, is one example. The name *dhow* is often used for a wide variety of ships used in the Arab world. Most dhows have one or two masts and lateen sails. Dhows were used for fishing and for trade. Dhows are still used in many parts of the Arab world today.

Another ship from Asia is the prau. The praus of Java were built with solid teak planks. The hull was supported by crossed boards in the planking and a wide, rectangular sail.

Below: A 19th-century engraving shows an Indonesian transport ship.

Top: A drawing shows a type of ship that was commonly seen along the coast of southern India during the 10th century. The ship could hold up to 200 passengers. Its sails were made of bamboo.

Above, center: A drawing shows a doni, a type of vessel used along the waters of the Arabian peninsula and along the eastern coast of Africa. Shipbuilders used cords made from vegetable and coconut fibers to attach the planks.

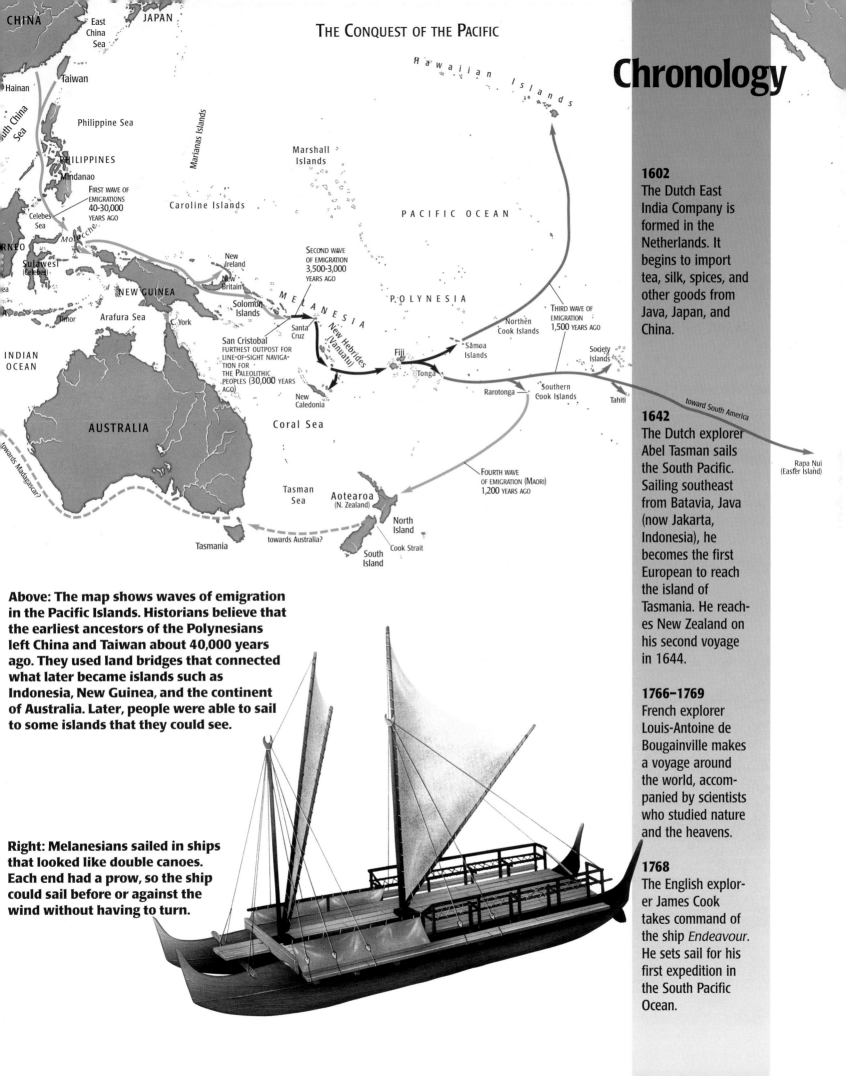

CHINA
East China Sea
JAPAN
Hainan
Taiwan
South China Sea
Philippine Sea
PHILIPPINES
Mindanao
Celebes Sea
Molucche
BORNEO
Sulawesi (Celebes)
NEW GUINEA
Timor
Arafura Sea
C. York

Marianas Islands
Marshall Islands
Caroline Islands
Hawaiian Islands
PACIFIC OCEAN

New Ireland
New Britain
MELANESIA
POLYNESIA
Solomon Islands
Santa Cruz
San Cristobal
New Hebrides (Vanuatu)
Fiji
Tonga
Northern Cook Islands
Sāmoa Islands
Society Islands
Tahiti
Southern Cook Islands
Rarotonga

New Caledonia

INDIAN OCEAN

AUSTRALIA

Coral Sea

Tasman Sea
Aotearoa (N. Zealand)
North Island
Cook Strait
South Island
Tasmania

FIRST WAVE OF EMIGRATIONS 40-30,000 YEARS AGO

SECOND WAVE OF EMIGRATION 3,500-3,000 YEARS AGO

THIRD WAVE OF EMIGRATION 1,500 YEARS AGO

FOURTH WAVE OF EMIGRATION (MAORI) 1,200 YEARS AGO

FURTHEST OUTPOST FOR LINE-OF-SIGHT NAVIGATION FOR THE PALEOLITHIC PEOPLES (30,000 YEARS AGO)

towards Madagascar?
towards Australia?
toward South America

Rapa Nui (Easter Island)

Above: The map shows waves of emigration in the Pacific Islands. Historians believe that the earliest ancestors of the Polynesians left China and Taiwan about 40,000 years ago. They used land bridges that connected what later became islands such as Indonesia, New Guinea, and the continent of Australia. Later, people were able to sail to some islands that they could see.

Right: Melanesians sailed in ships that looked like double canoes. Each end had a prow, so the ship could sail before or against the wind without having to turn.

Chronology

1602
The Dutch East India Company is formed in the Netherlands. It begins to import tea, silk, spices, and other goods from Java, Japan, and China.

1642
The Dutch explorer Abel Tasman sails the South Pacific. Sailing southeast from Batavia, Java (now Jakarta, Indonesia), he becomes the first European to reach the island of Tasmania. He reaches New Zealand on his second voyage in 1644.

1766–1769
French explorer Louis-Antoine de Bougainville makes a voyage around the world, accompanied by scientists who studied nature and the heavens.

1768
The English explorer James Cook takes command of the ship *Endeavour*. He sets sail for his first expedition in the South Pacific Ocean.

In China

Ancient Chinese merchant and fighting ships were called "junks." A junk had a large hull with watertight compartments below. This would prevent it from sinking if a leak appeared. A junk had square sails and up to five masts. In the early years the sails were made of mats. Later the sails were made of canvas that was reinforced with mats.

Marco Polo, a famous 13th-century Venetian traveler who spent many years in China, gave others a lot of information about the junks of ancient China. Historians have found that for hundreds of years, the design of junks changed very little. Junks sailing in the late 19th century and the early 20th century had many features in common with those Marco Polo saw.

Right: A drawing shows a junk that is used to carry tourists around the bay of Shanghai.

Below: A drawing shows a large Chinese junk. The sail is made of vegetable fibers that are supported by bamboo slats.

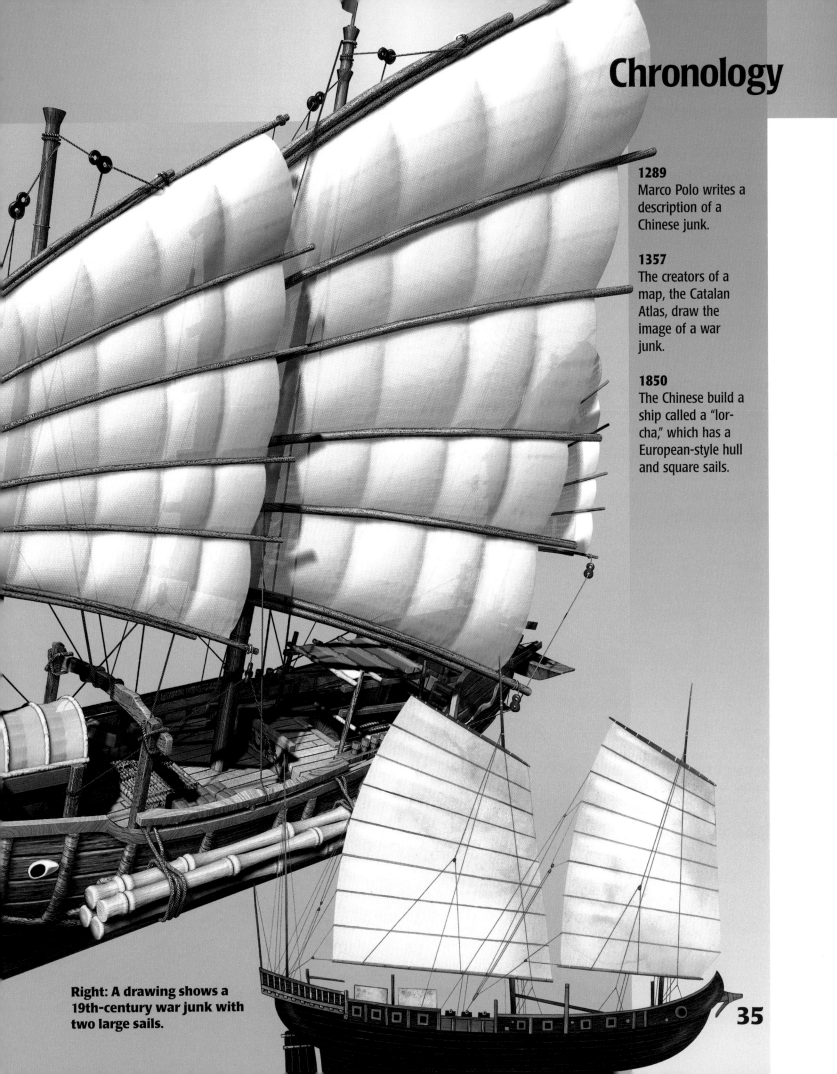

1289
Marco Polo writes a description of a Chinese junk.

1357
The creators of a map, the Catalan Atlas, draw the image of a war junk.

1850
The Chinese build a ship called a "lorcha," which has a European-style hull and square sails.

Right: A drawing shows a 19th-century war junk with two large sails.

Galleys

A type of ship called a "galley" began to be used around the end of the 14th century. The galleys of this era had oars arranged along one level. Three to five men powered each oar on large galleys. The oars were lined up along the length of the ship. The galley had a unique pointed prow that offered a way for people to board the ship. It was also used as a weapon.

In the 14th century, shipbuilders created a type of ship called a "galleass." The galleass was a large, fast galley. Mediterranean countries used the galleass as a warship during the 16th and 17th centuries. A galleass had both sails and oars, but the oars provided the main source of power to move the ship.

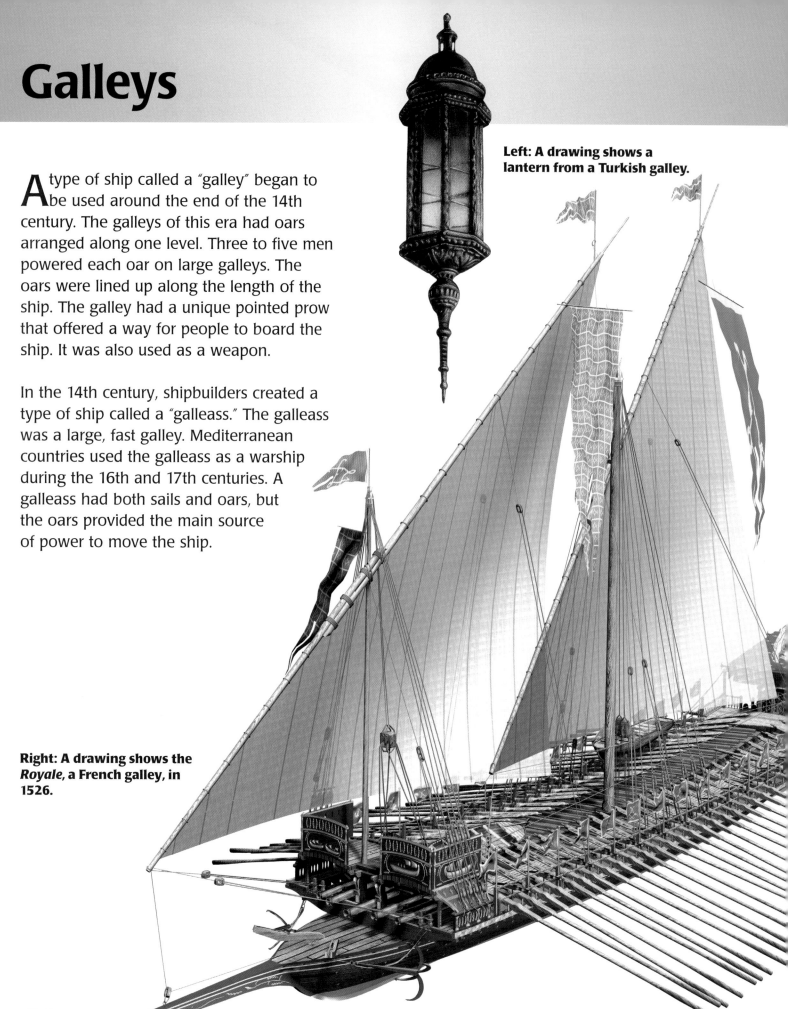

Left: A drawing shows a lantern from a Turkish galley.

Right: A drawing shows the *Royale*, a French galley, in 1526.

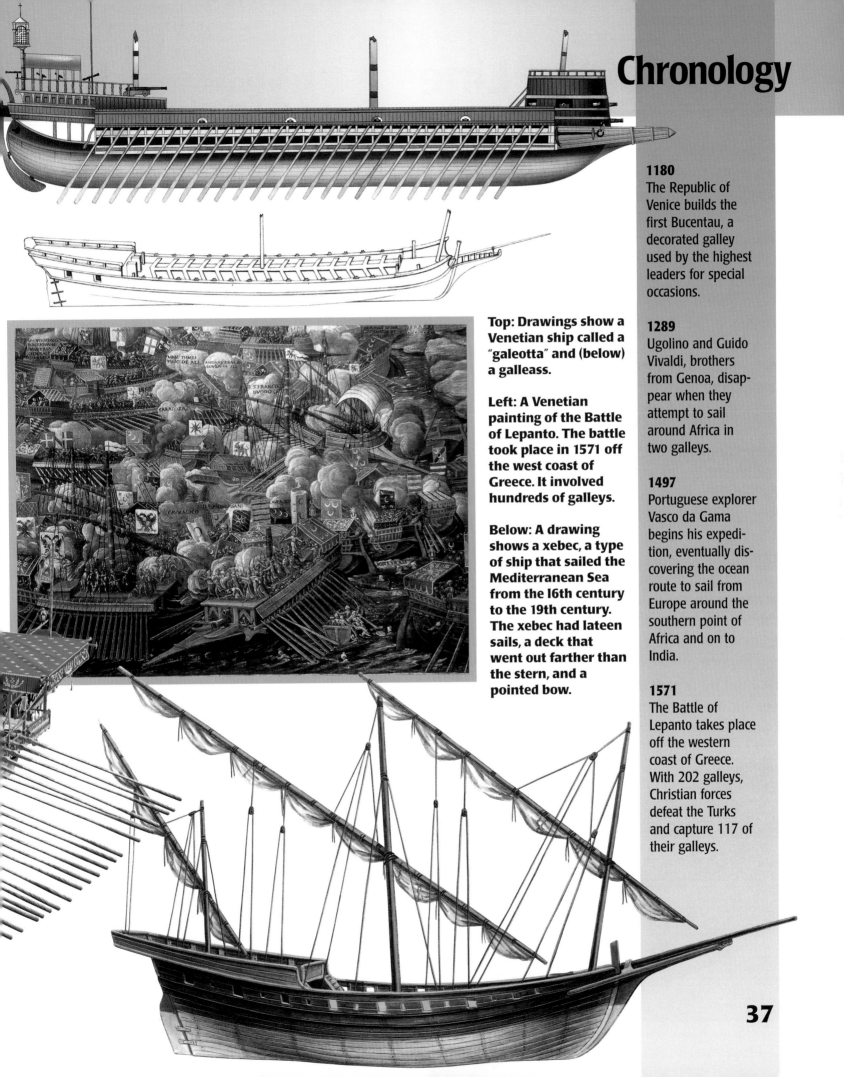

Top: Drawings show a Venetian ship called a "galeotta" and (below) a galleass.

Left: A Venetian painting of the Battle of Lepanto. The battle took place in 1571 off the west coast of Greece. It involved hundreds of galleys.

Below: A drawing shows a xebec, a type of ship that sailed the Mediterranean Sea from the 16th century to the 19th century. The xebec had lateen sails, a deck that went out farther than the stern, and a pointed bow.

1180
The Republic of Venice builds the first Bucentau, a decorated galley used by the highest leaders for special occasions.

1289
Ugolino and Guido Vivaldi, brothers from Genoa, disappear when they attempt to sail around Africa in two galleys.

1497
Portuguese explorer Vasco da Gama begins his expedition, eventually discovering the ocean route to sail from Europe around the southern point of Africa and on to India.

1571
The Battle of Lepanto takes place off the western coast of Greece. With 202 galleys, Christian forces defeat the Turks and capture 117 of their galleys.

Ships of the Line

In the 17th century, ship construction improved again as people learned how to make better sails and how to fit new ships with many powerful weapons. The new design of ship was called the "ship of the line." It was a type of sailing warship that became the backbone of the world's great navies at the time. The ships usually had three masts. They carried as many as 100 cannons, which were arranged on three decks. The walls of the ships were very thick and could withstand the impact of cannon fire. European navies used these ships to fight battles that might involve more than 100 ships and last for days.

The name for these ships came from the way they were used in wars. In naval battles, commanders began trying new tactics with these ships. They commanded their ships to form a line, so that they could fight the enemy without fearing that they might be fired on by one of the friendly ships. So, a ship powerful enough to stand in the line of battle became known as a ship of the line.

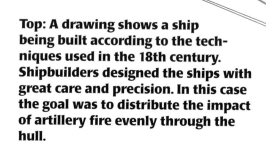

Top: A drawing shows a ship being built according to the techniques used in the 18th century. Shipbuilders designed the ships with great care and precision. In this case the goal was to distribute the impact of artillery fire evenly through the hull.

Above: A drawing shows the hull of a ship of the line under construction.

Left: A drawing shows the framework of an 18th-century French ship of the line.

Right: Ships of the line were warships. Some examples of the provisions and tools that were needed on such ships include a barrel to hold gunpowder (1), a charge chamber (2), a powder horn (3), and ramrods (4, 5, and 6).

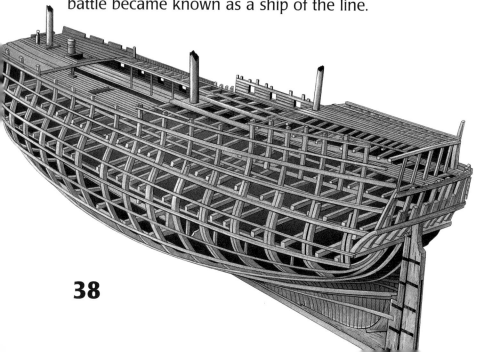

Chronology

Powder Barrel 100

1

2

3

4 5 6

Above: *Victory*, flagship of the English fleet in the Mediterranean from 1793, was a first-rate ship of the line. It had a crew of more than 800 men and its decks held 100 cannons. On the gun deck were 30 cannons that fired 42-pound balls. The middle deck held 28 cannons that fired 24-pound balls. The 30 cannons on the upper deck fired 12-pound balls. On the quarterdeck and forecastle were 12 cannons that fired 12-pound balls. A cutaway of one of Victory's heavy cannons (above right) shows the ball projectile inside the cylinder of the gun mount.

39

Frigates, Brigantines, and Schooners

In the 18th century, the ships of the line were replaced with new designs. Shipbuilders began to build ships that were smaller and easier to steer. Their new ships were the frigate, the brigantine, and the schooner.

The frigate was fast and had many sails set between masts. The sails made the frigate easier to control than any of the earlier ship designs. The brigantine had two masts with square sails. The schooner was a type of sailing ship that had two or more masts, each with what were called "fore-and-aft sails." That is, there were sails extending forward from the masts and behind them. During the American Revolution, the American colonies used many schooners in their war for independence from Great Britain.

Above: Captain James Cook, an English explorer, took his third scientific journey in the Austral Islands in 1776 aboard the frigate *Discovery*.

Top, left: The figurehead from the English brigantine *Benmore* was repainted with the American flag after the ship was sold to American owners.

Below: The *Bounty*, a frigate in the English navy, was launched in 1787. It became famous for the mutiny that took place later in Tahiti. A mutiny happens when sailors onboard a ship refuse to obey the orders of those in charge.

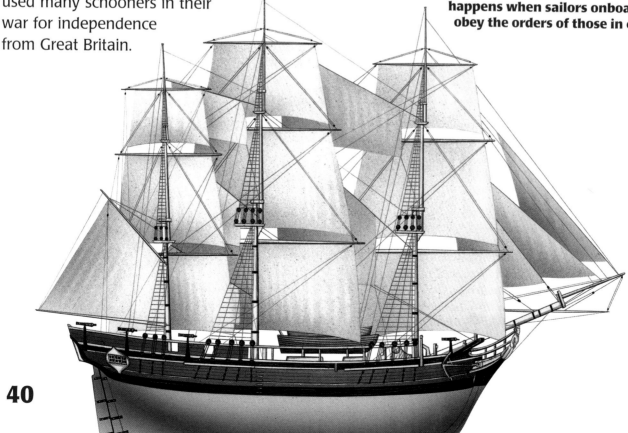

Above: A drawing shows the frigate *Constitution*, one of six ships of the first fleet of the United States. The ship is now berthed in Boston.

Right: Ships are defined by the number of masts they have and the shape and location of their sails. Pictured are schooners (1 and 2), a brigantine (3), a sailing ship called a "bark" (4), a xebec (5), and a type of sailing ship called a "barkentine" (6).

Below: Drawings show a ship that brought slaves from Africa to North America, and a diagram of how the slaves were arranged in the ship's hold.

1646
The first frigate is constructed in English shipyards.

1670
The stay sail appears. The stay sail is a piece of cloth with one or two sides attached to the ropes or wires that hold the mast in place.

1789
The mutiny of the *Bounty*, a frigate of the British navy, takes place.

1794
The U.S. Congress authorizes the construction of six frigates for a navy.

1815
The frigate is the most common ship in European navies.

1860
The invention of steamships brings the age of great sailing ships to an end.

Fluyts and Clippers

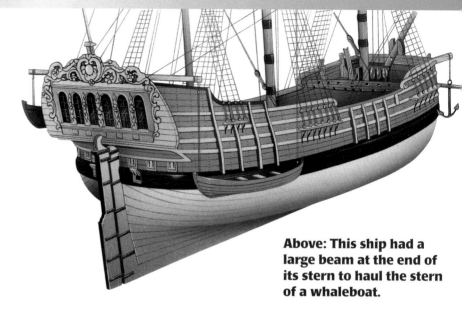

One of the most important merchant and fishing vessels in northern Europe was the fluyt. (The word is pronounced like "flight.") It was a narrow ship with a round stern. Its sides slanted inward. The fluyt was created in the Netherlands in the 17th century. It was designed to have as much space as possible for cargo. The Dutch used fluyts to hunt whales.

The clipper was a very fast ship with many sails that was used in the 19th century. Clippers were long and narrow, and designed to be fast. The British and the Americans built most of the clippers. Their masts had so many sails that they were said to form a cloud in the air. One clipper ship was even named the *Flying Cloud*. Clipper ships sailed all over the world. They were used on trade routes between Britain and China. During California's gold rush, they sailed from San Francisco, around the southernmost islands of South America, and to New York.

Above: This ship had a large beam at the end of its stern to haul the stern of a whaleboat.

Below: A drawing shows a model ship in a bottle.

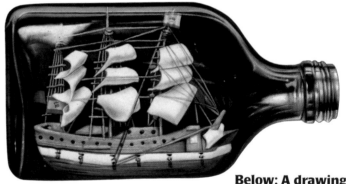

Below: A drawing shows a figurehead from the ship, the *Finmarken*, from the Maritime Museum in Bergen, Norway.

Below: Whaling was a difficult and dangerous way to make a living.

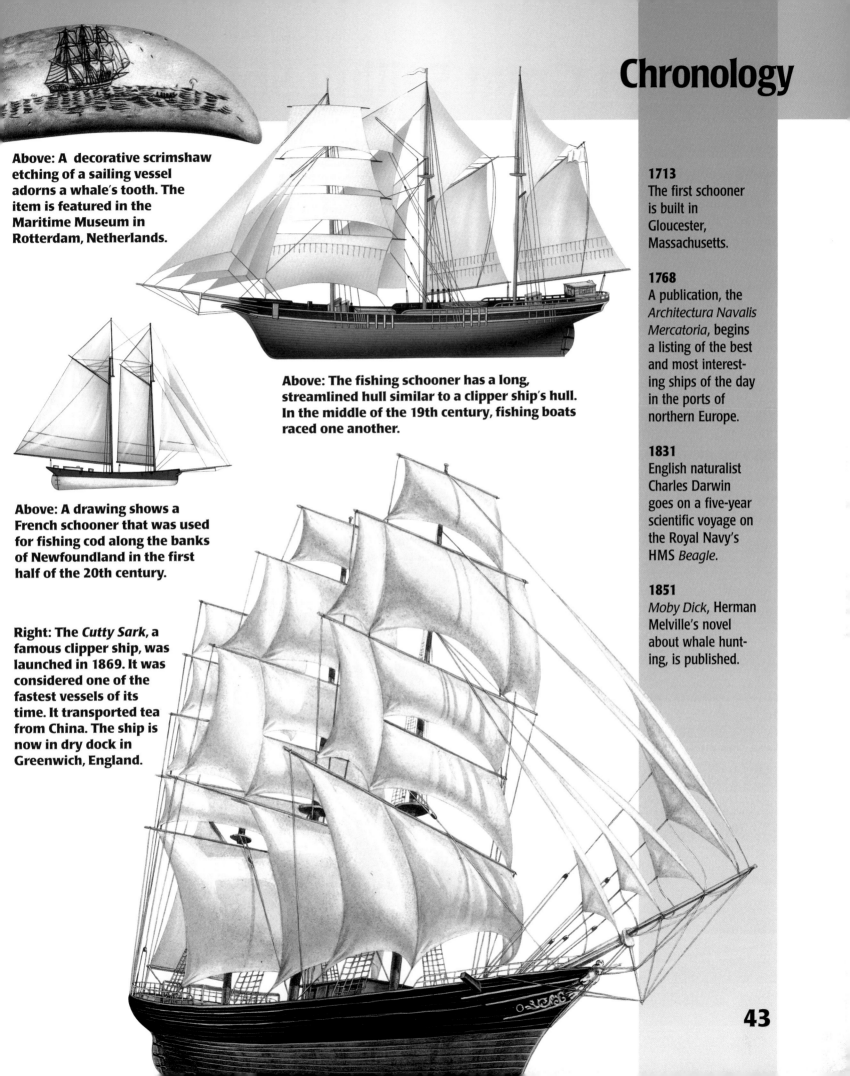

Chronology

Above: A decorative scrimshaw etching of a sailing vessel adorns a whale's tooth. The item is featured in the Maritime Museum in Rotterdam, Netherlands.

Above: The fishing schooner has a long, streamlined hull similar to a clipper ship's hull. In the middle of the 19th century, fishing boats raced one another.

Above: A drawing shows a French schooner that was used for fishing cod along the banks of Newfoundland in the first half of the 20th century.

Right: The *Cutty Sark*, a famous clipper ship, was launched in 1869. It was considered one of the fastest vessels of its time. It transported tea from China. The ship is now in dry dock in Greenwich, England.

1713
The first schooner is built in Gloucester, Massachusetts.

1768
A publication, the *Architectura Navalis Mercatoria*, begins a listing of the best and most interesting ships of the day in the ports of northern Europe.

1831
English naturalist Charles Darwin goes on a five-year scientific voyage on the Royal Navy's HMS *Beagle*.

1851
Moby Dick, Herman Melville's novel about whale hunting, is published.

The Last Great Sailing Ships

The age of sail, the time when the great sailing ships dominated the seas, ended in the 19th century. The invention of the steamship meant that sail power was no longer needed. In 1862 a naval battle that took place during the American Civil War off the coast of Virginia marked the end of the great wooden sailing ships. The battle between the *Monitor*, a ship of the Union forces, and the *Virginia*, a Confederate ship, was the first fight between two ironclad ships. After that battle, shipbuilding and naval warfare changed. The great sailing ships on the oceans today are either tourist attractions or training ships that teach sailing techniques.

Above: The German *Preussen* had five masts with 47 sails. It was launched in 1902.

Below: The *Thomas Lawson* had seven masts. The American ship was launched in 1902, but it wrecked two years later in the English Channel.

Right: The *Amerigo Vespucci* is a training ship for the Italian Naval Academy. It was launched in 1931.

1819
The American *Savannah* becomes the first steam-powered ship to cross the Atlantic Ocean.

1869
A man-made waterway called the Suez Canal opens. It connects the Red Sea with the Mediterranean Sea and reduces the miles a ship would need to travel.

1921
The famed Bordes company of Nantes keeps a fleet of sailing vessels to transport wheat from Australia.

1949
The *Pamir*, a Finnish ship, becomes the last windjammer to sail commercially around Cape Horn. Windjammers are huge sailboats with four masts and steel hulls.

Glossary

aft: the rear end of the ship.

bireme: an ancient galley ship with two banks of oars on each side.

bow: the forward end of the ship.

brigantine: a sailing ship with two masts and square sails.

caravel built: boatbuilding that uses planks on the hull that are laid side by side. It was a typical boat in the Mediterranean Sea.

castle: a structure on ships that rises above the bow or the stern of the ship.

dhow: a name for a wide variety of sailing ships that are used in the Red Sea and Indian Ocean.

draft: the depth of a ship's keel below the water.

figurehead: an ornamental figure on a ship's bow.

frigate: a medium-sized warship with square sails used in the 18th and 19th centuries.

galleass: a large, fast warship with three masts used in the Mediterranean Sea during the 16th and 17th centuries.

galleon: a large three-masted sailing ship with square sails and usually two or more decks.

Galleons were used from the 15th to the 17th centuries for trade and for war, especially by the Spanish.

galley: a large ship powered by sails and oars that was used in ancient times in the Mediterranean Sea.

hold: the interior of a ship below its deck that is used to store cargo.

hull: the main body of the ship, excluding any masts, sails, or motors.

isthmus: a narrow strip of land that connects two larger pieces of land. An isthmus has water on both sides.

keel: the main structural beam of a ship, running from the prow to the stern, around which the frame is built.

junk: a flat-bottomed ship that has been used in China since ancient times.

lateen sail: a sail that is shaped like a triangle.

latitude: the position north or south of Earth's equator, measured in degrees on a map or globe.

mast: a pole that extends upward from a ship's deck that is used to support sails.

naturalist: someone who studies plant and animal life.

Phoenicians: people who lived on the eastern coast of the Mediterranean Sea in ancient times. Skillful sailors, they founded many trading colonies. Carthage was their most famous colony.

prow: the forward part of a ship.

Punic Wars: the three wars waged by the Romans against Carthage between 264 B.C. and 146 B.C. The Punic Wars ended with the destruction of Carthage.

rudder: a hinged plate that is attached at the rear of the ship and is used to steer the ship.

schooner: a ship with two or more masts and sails that are set lengthwise.

stern: the rear part of a ship.

trireme: an ancient galley ship with three banks of oars on each side.

xebec: a small ship with three masts that used triangular and square sails and sailed on the Mediterranean Sea.

For More Information

Andrea Hopkins, *Vikings: The Norse Discovery of America*. New York: PowerKids Press, 2002.

Mervyn D. Kaufman, *Christopher Columbus*. Mankato, MN: Capstone, 2004.

Andrew Langley, *100 Things You Should Know About Pirates*. Broomall, PA: Mason Crest, 2003.

Fiona MacDonald, *You Wouldn't Want to Sail with Christopher Columbus*. New York: Franklin Watts, 2004.

Susan M. Margeson, *Viking*. New York: Dorling Kindersley, 2000.

Earle Rice, *Sir Francis Drake: Navigator and Pirate*. New York: Benchmark Books/Marshall Cavendish, 2003.

Jeremy Thornton, *The Birth of the American Navy*. New York: Rosen, 2003.

Aileen Weintraub, *Vikings and Explorers*. Danbury, CT: Children's Press, 2005.

David West, *Christopher Columbus: The Life of a Master Navigator and Explorer*. New York: Rosen, 2005.

Laura Lee Wren, *Pirates and Privateers of the High Seas*. Berkeley Heights, NJ: Enslow, 2002.

Index